MAPLE M. BEAR

...a mama bear
who is sweet and
kind and full
of hugs - as bears
and mamas
should be

HICKORY B. BEAR

... a small boy bear
who is often quite
serious and very,
very proud to be
a bear

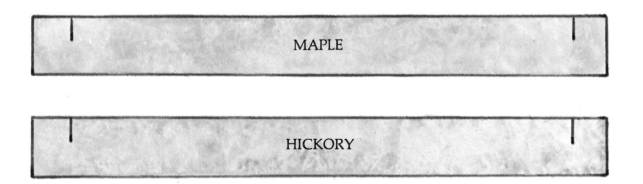

MAPLE

HICKORY

Maple M. Bear and Hickory B. Bear

Plate 1

CHESTNUT P. BEAR

...a papa bear who is
distinguished, wise and
gentle – a good and
heroic bear

JUNIPER G. BEAR

... a very small girl bear
who is somewhat shy but
bright and clever for a
bear of so few years

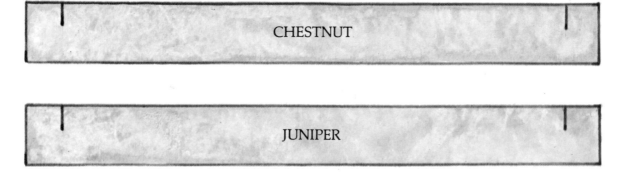

CHESTNUT

JUNIPER

Chestnut P. Bear and Juniper G. Bear

Plate 2

Papa Bear is fond of birds and likes to build houses for his little friends.

A long time ago Papa was in the Navy. He has grown just a little since then but can still fit into his uniform. He has many medals for bravery and likes to wear them on special occasions.

carpenter clothes

naval uniform

Papa's nightshirt and cookies

Papa's bow tie

Some of Chestnut P. Bear's Everyday Clothes

Plate 3

Mama's ribbon

Mama Bear likes to make soft, warm bear quilts for cold winter nights. This is her favorite design. It is called "Bear Paw."

house dress

going-to-market dress

Mama's sewing basket

Little bears do not always like to go to bed, but they love to listen to bedtime stories read by mama. They like to hear about fairies and elves, good children and small bears.

Mama's market hat with violets (slash along dotted line)

Robe

Some of Maple M. Bear's Everyday Clothes

Plate 4

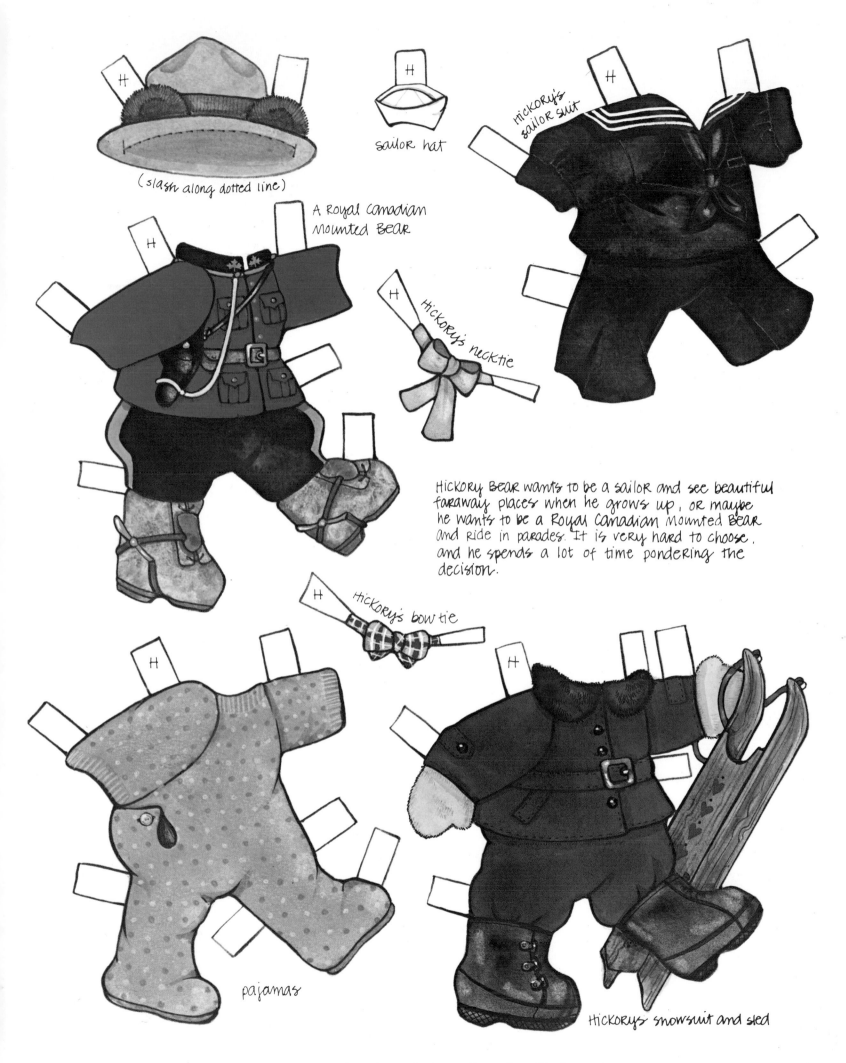

(slash along dotted line)

sailor hat

Hickory's sailor suit

A Royal Canadian Mounted Bear

Hickory's necktie

Hickory Bear wants to be a sailor and see beautiful faraway places when he grows up, or maybe he wants to be a Royal Canadian Mounted Bear and ride in parades. It is very hard to choose, and he spends a lot of time pondering the decision.

Hickory's bow tie

pajamas

Hickory's snowsuit and sled

Some of Hickory B. Bear's Everyday Clothes

Plate 5

Fall is Juniper's favorite time of year. Brightly colored leaves fall and swoosh around her as she walks to school.

school dress

winter hat and coat

hair bows

Junipers ribbon

Juniper collects leaves

(slash along dotted line)

Juniper jumps rope

(cut out)

(slash along dotted line)

a sailor girl bear

a rain slicker and hat

nightgown

small girl bears (and their frogs) like rain, too. It smells so good.

Some of Juniper G. Bear's Everyday Clothes

Plate 6

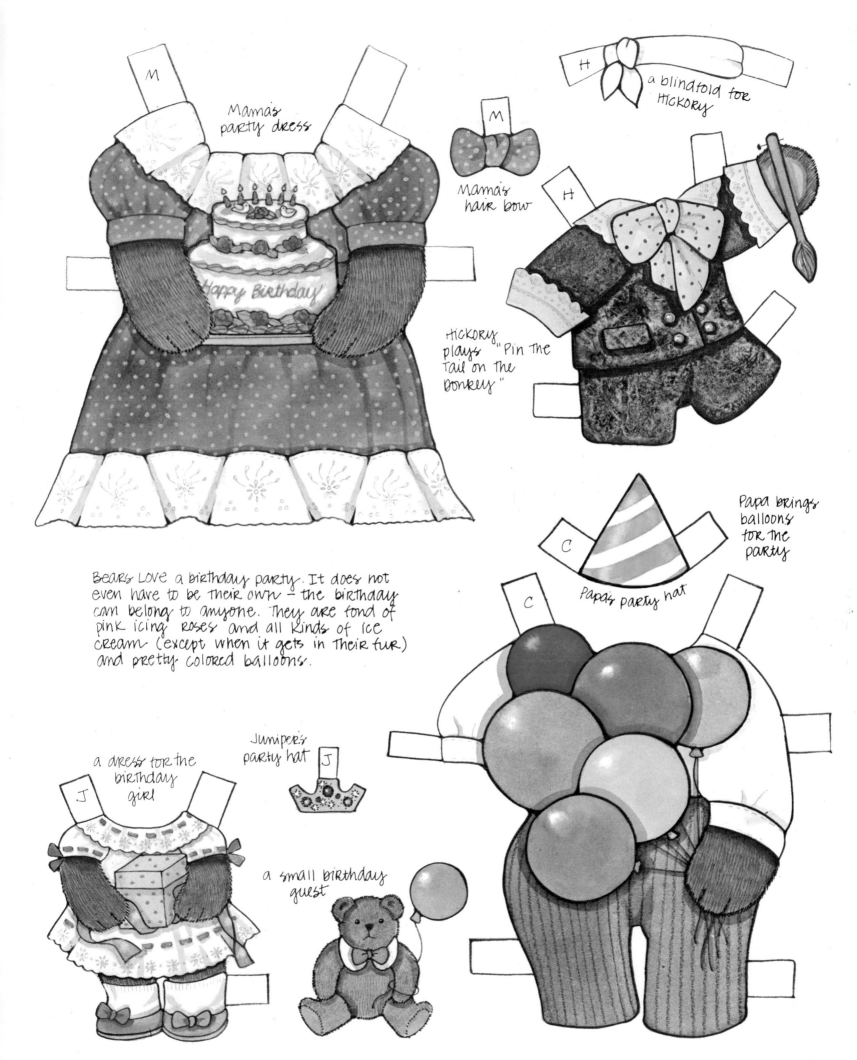

Mama's party dress

a blindfold for HICKORY

Mama's hair bow

Hickory plays "Pin The Tail on the Donkey"

Papa brings balloons for the party

Papa's party hat

Bears LOVE a birthday party. It does not even have to be their own — the birthday can belong to anyone. They are fond of pink icing roses and all kinds of ice cream (except when it gets in their fur) and pretty colored balloons.

Juniper's party hat

a dress for the birthday girl

a small birthday guest

The Bears Have a Birthday Party

Plate 7

costume for Mama – the trapeze bear!

M

Hickory's strong bear outfit

M

mama's hat

H

The bears went to the circus once when they lived in the big city.

J

They saw huge elephants and very small ponies and silly clowns and ate LOTS of cotton candy. Sometimes the bears fancy that they have joined the circus and are star performers.

(stash along dotted line)

C

Ringmaster's clothes for Papa

Juniper's clown hat and suit

J

a circus dog

The Bears Pretend to Be in the Circus

Plate 8

M

a Navajo bear's dress

H

outfit for a cowboy dude bear

Hickory's cowboy hat

H

(slash along dotted line)

Papa's hat

C

(slash along dotted line)

Male bears think they look very grand dressed as a cowboy or sheriff, but lady bears would rather wear pretty Indian dresses with fine ornaments and brilliant colored beads.

C

Papa's sheriff outfit

J

Papa has been to Montana, so he thinks he is best qualified to be the sheriff. He feels rather important wearing his badge.

a Cheyenne bear

The Bears Play Cowboys and Indians

Plate 9

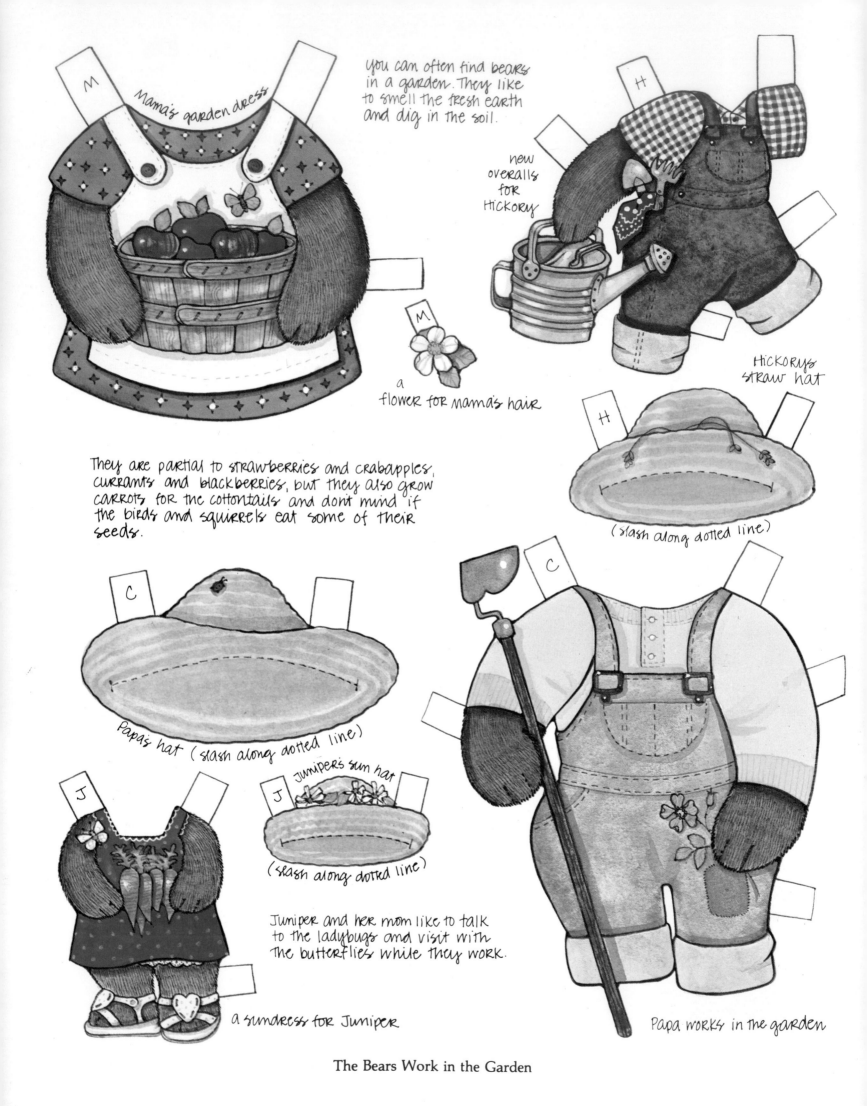

M

Mama's garden dress

You can often find bears in a garden. They like to smell the fresh earth and dig in the soil.

new overalls for Hickory

H

M

a flower for mama's hair

Hickory's straw hat

H

(slash along dotted line)

They are partial to strawberries and crabapples, currants and blackberries, but they also grow carrots for the cottontails and don't mind if the birds and squirrels eat some of their seeds.

C

Papa's hat (slash along dotted line)

C

J

Juniper's sun hat

J

(slash along dotted line)

Juniper and her mom like to talk to the ladybugs and visit with the butterflies while they work.

a sundress for Juniper

Papa works in the garden

The Bears Work in the Garden

Plate 10

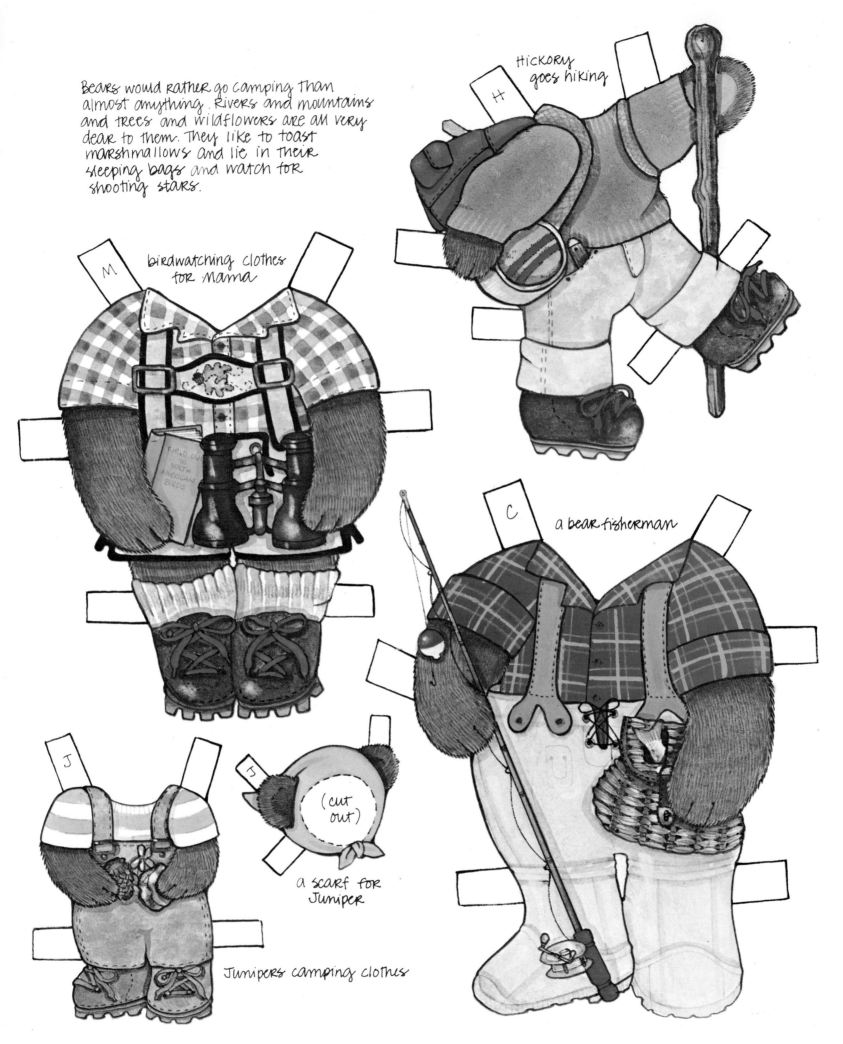

Bears would rather go camping than almost anything. Rivers and mountains and trees and wildflowers are all very dear to them. They like to toast marshmallows and lie in their sleeping bags and watch for shooting stars.

Hickory goes hiking

birdwatching clothes for Mama

a bear fisherman

(cut out)

a scarf for Juniper

Junipers camping clothes

The Bears Go Camping

Plate 11

Mama's swim dress

Mama's swim hat
(slash along dotted line)

Hickory's swimsuit

Nothing feels better to bears than warm sand between their toes! Bears never tire of listening for the sea in seashells and believe that the sparkles on the water are diamonds.

(slash along dotted line)
A sunhat for Mama

Juniper's inner tube horse
(slash along dotted line)

Juniper's sandcastle

(cut out)
Juniper's swim cap

Juniper can't swim very well but builds wonderfully fine castles of sand and likes to float about in her inner tube.

Papa's swimsuit

a sunsuit for Juniper

The Bears Go to the Seashore

Plate 12

Mama's gypsy outfit

M

H

Hickory—
a hobo bear

Mama's gypsy scarf

M

(slash along dotted line)

C

Papa's scarecrow hat (slash along dotted line)

Lots of people think bears are scary, but really they're not. They would rather be friendly and like Halloween mostly because they can eat shiny red candy apples and saltwater taffy and carve funny pumpkin faces.

C

a scarecrow bear

a good witch dress and hat

J

(slash along dotted line)

J

a ghost bear

The Bears Dress Up for Halloween

Plate 13

M a Queen bear

(cut out)

H a knight bear

H Hickory's hat

C clothes for a Robin Hood-type bear

The bears would have liked to live in medieval times — B.T.B. (Before Teddy Bears). They would love to see a REAL castle and become enchanted bears like the ones in the fairy tales. HICKORY is positive he had royal ancestors — surely at least one who was a glorious knight.

(cut out)

a lady-in-waiting bear with her enchanted frog

The Bears Pretend It Is the Middle Ages

Plate 14

Russian peasant dress and babushka for Mama

Hickory's German hat

(slash along dotted line)

(cut out)

M

M

M

H

German clothes for Hickory

C

a scottish outfit for Papa

J

Bears like to dress in costumes from other countries - it makes them feel closer to bears living in distant parts of the world.

a little Dutch bear

The Bears Dress in Their Folk Costumes

Plate 15

Christmas is a favorite holiday for bears. They like sugar cookies with red and green sprinkles and shiny glass ornaments, big fluffy snowflakes and fir tree smells that remind them of when they lived in the forest.

an elf vest

an elf hat for Hickory

(slash along dotted line)

Mama bakes cookies for Christmas

Juniper's halo

(cut out)

It is a time for everyone to be friends – bears and men and all creatures of the earth.

a santa bear

clothes for an angel bear

The Bears Celebrate Christmas

Plate 16